Cambridge English Readers

Level 1

Series editor: Philip Prowse

The Caribbean File

Richard MacAndrew

CAMBRIDGE
UNIVERSITY PRESS

CAMBRIDGE
UNIVERSITY PRESS

University Printing House, Cambridge CB2 8BS, United Kingdom

One Liberty Plaza, 20th Floor, New York, NY 10006, USA

477 Williamstown Road, Port Melbourne, VIC 3207, Australia

4843/24, 2nd Floor, Ansari Road, Daryaganj, Delhi – 110002, India

79 Anson Road, #06–04/06, Singapore 079906

Cambridge University Press is part of the University of Cambridge.

It furthers the University's mission by disseminating knowledge in the pursuit of education, learning and research at the highest international levels of excellence.

www.cambridge.org
Information on this title: www.cambridge.org/9781107674257

© Cambridge University Press 2013

First published 2013
Reprinted 2017

Richard MacAndrew has asserted his right to be identified as the Author
of the Work in accordance with the Copyright, Designs and Patents Act 1988.

Printed and bound in the United Kingdom by Hobbs the Printers Ltd
Typeset by Aptara Inc.
Map artwork by Malcolm Barnes
Illustrations by Paul Dickinson

A catalogue record of this book is available from the British Library

ISBN 978-1-107-674257 paperback

Contents

People in the story

Ian Munro: a British agent
Naylor: Munro's boss
Sam Tajik: a terrorist
Jonas Beck: a terrorist
Maria Salgado: Jonas Beck's old girlfriend
Patrick Anderson: a nuclear scientist
Jamie Anderson: Patrick Anderson's son
Wesley Samuels: a police officer

The Caribbean

N

Florida

Mexico

Cuba

Jamaica

ATLANTIC

OCEAN

CARIBBEAN SEA

St
Kitts

Tobago

Venezuela

Chapter 1   *Two dangerous men*

'Take a look at these,' said Naylor.

He put two photos in front of Munro. Two men. There were names on the photos. One man was dark, Asian maybe. His name was Sam Tajik. The second man looked European – German or Scandinavian. Jonas Beck.

'Sam Tajik. Jonas Beck,' said Naylor. 'Dangerous men. Terrorists.'

Munro waited. He worked for Naylor. And Naylor never gave him easy jobs.

'Yesterday I had an email from our man in the Caribbean,' said Naylor. 'He saw these two men at the same table in the same hotel.'

Naylor showed Munro a third photo. Beck and Tajik were in a hotel restaurant. Naylor looked up at Munro.

'I'm not happy,' he said. 'Beck always works in Europe – so what's he doing in the Caribbean? Having a holiday? No. He's not.'

Naylor looked down at Tajik's photo.

'And Tajik is an animal, a killer,' he said. 'He hates Americans. He hates Europeans. He hates the West. Why is he talking to Beck? What's he doing in the same room as Beck?'

Naylor sat back.

'They're talking and laughing and having a good time. They're "friends". I don't like it.'

'Where in the Caribbean are they?' asked Munro.

'Tobago,' replied Naylor. 'At the Mount Irvine Bay Hotel. That's where you're going. There's a room for you at the hotel from tomorrow night.'

There was a file on the table: 'The Caribbean File'. Naylor put the photos into the file and gave it to Munro.

'Take this and read it,' he said. 'Go. Watch. Listen. Why are they there? What are they doing? I want some answers.'

* * *

At six o'clock the next evening Munro got out of a taxi in front of the Mount Irvine Bay Hotel. He loved the Caribbean: the sun, the sea, the palm trees, the friendly people. He walked into the hotel.

'You have a room for me,' Munro told the receptionist. 'The name's Munro.'

The receptionist looked on his computer. Just then a woman came into the hotel behind Munro.

He turned to look at her.

She was beautiful – tall, with short dark hair and dark eyes.

Munro smiled at her.

'Hi,' he said.

'Hello.' She smiled warmly back.

The receptionist looked up.

'Excuse me,' the woman said to Munro. Then she said to the receptionist, 'I'd like some tea in my room, please.'

'Of course, Ms Salgado,' he replied. 'Two minutes.'

'Argentina or Uruguay?' Munro asked Salgado.

Salgado looked at him, a question in her eyes.

'Your English is very good,' said Munro, 'but I think you're from Argentina or maybe Uruguay.'

'Ah!' said Salgado. 'Well, you're right.' She smiled at Munro again. 'I am from one of those countries.' And she turned and walked away.

'Nice answer!' thought Munro, and he laughed.

* * *

At seven o'clock Beck and Tajik were back in the hotel restaurant. This time Munro was at a table near them. The two men talked and laughed. They spoke in English.

Munro read the *Tobago News*. But he also watched and listened. He heard a little of the conversation, but Beck and Tajik didn't talk about anything important. After dinner they asked for coffee.

Just then Salgado walked into the restaurant.

'She is very beautiful,' thought Munro.

Salgado saw Munro. He smiled at her. She smiled back.

Beck and Tajik saw her and stopped talking.

Beck said something to Tajik, something about Salgado. And they laughed.

Salgado gave Beck a long angry look. Then she turned and left.

Beck laughed again, but it wasn't a nice laugh.

Munro thought about Beck. What did he say about Salgado? Was it just 'man talk' with Tajik? Or did he know her?

Beck and Tajik finished their coffee and left the restaurant.

Munro went to the bar. There were ten or twelve people there. Munro asked for a Carib beer and sat down with his back to the wall. He always sat with his back to the wall. No one can come up behind you.

There was cricket on the television. West Indians love to play and watch cricket. Munro watched the television, drank his beer and thought again about the two men. Why were they here?

'Do you understand cricket?'

The question came from Munro's left. He turned. It was Ms Salgado.

'A little,' replied Munro. 'But it's an English sport, and I'm Scottish.'

'Ah!' said Salgado.

Munro smiled at Salgado.

'Can I get you a drink?' he asked.

Salgado looked round the room. 'Not here. There are too many people,' she said. 'But there's some whisky in my room. That's from Scotland too, I think.'

They left the bar and walked to Salgado's room. She opened the door.

'Do you know those two men in the restaurant?' asked Munro.

Salgado put a finger to his lips.

'Sh!' she said. 'We don't want to talk about them.' Then her lips met his and Munro felt the fire in her body.

＊　＊　＊

Munro opened his eyes. He heard a noise. Maria Salgado came out of the bathroom in a black T-shirt and jeans.

'What time is it?' asked Munro.

'I'm late,' said Salgado.

'Where are you going?' asked Munro.

Again Salgado put a finger to Munro's lips.

'Goodbye, Ian,' she said. 'I enjoyed meeting you.'

She left the room quickly.

Munro looked at his watch. It was five o'clock in the morning. He looked round Salgado's room. There were no bags, no clothes, nothing of Salgado's in the room. Just his clothes on a chair.

Munro dressed quickly and ran to the front of the hotel. He was too late. He saw Salgado get into a black car and drive away. There were also two men in the car. Beck and Tajik.

Chapter 2 *A call to Naylor*

Munro ran back into the hotel. The receptionist was at his computer.

'Those people in the black car,' said Munro. 'Where are they going?'

'I don't know,' answered the receptionist.

Munro put $50 next to the receptionist's computer.

'They put their bags in a taxi and told the driver to go to the airport,' said the receptionist. He took the $50. 'Then they got into that black car. But I don't know where they're going.'

'I need a taxi to the airport,' said Munro. 'Can you call me one?'

'Of course,' replied the receptionist.

Munro ran back to his room for his bag. By five forty-five he was at Crown Point International Airport. There was a plane to Trinidad at six-forty. Munro sat down to watch and wait. He took out his phone. It was two o'clock in the morning in London.

'Naylor.'

'When does Naylor sleep?' thought Munro. 'I'm at the airport,' he said. 'Beck and Tajik have got a woman with them. Her name's Maria Salgado …'

'Salgado!' said Naylor.

'Yes,' said Munro. 'She's tall with …'

'I know,' said Naylor. 'She's a terrorist too. I don't like this at all. She was Beck's girlfriend for five years. Then she left him and went back to South America. He was very angry about that. At the time he told people he wanted to kill her. But I don't think she knew about that. Why is Beck talking to her again? This isn't good.'

A plane came in from Trinidad. People got out and walked into the airport. A black car drove out to a small blue plane next to the one from Trinidad. Two men and a woman got out. Beck, Tajik and Salgado. Then a boy got out too.

'Wait a minute,' said Munro to Naylor.

Munro looked at the boy. He was twelve or thirteen years old and wore jeans and a light blue shirt. He looked half asleep.

Salgado took the boy's hand. They walked slowly to the plane. The boy got in, then the terrorists. The plane started to move.

'They just got here,' Munro told Naylor. 'Beck, Tajik and Salgado. And they've got a boy with them. They're just leaving on a small plane. The boy's about twelve or thirteen. White. Blue shirt. Jeans. Short brown hair.'

'How did he look?' asked Naylor.

'OK,' replied Munro, 'but he moved slowly. He looked half asleep.'

'What are the letters on the plane?' asked Naylor.

'G-BUTY,' answered Munro.

'Give me ten minutes,' said Naylor.

Munro bought a coffee and waited for Naylor's call. It took fifteen minutes.

'I spoke to the airport,' said Naylor. 'They're going to St Kitts. You're on the next plane to Trinidad. You go from there to Antigua, and then to St Kitts. Get to St Kitts and find them. And get me a photo of the boy. I need to see him.'

Chapter 3 *A photo for Naylor*

Munro got to St Kitts at five forty-five in the afternoon. It was still hot and sunny. A large police officer in a light brown shirt and trousers came up to him.

'You must be Ian Munro,' said the police officer. 'I'm Wesley Samuels of the St Kitts Police.'

'Nice to meet you,' said Munro.

'Mr Naylor asked me to help you,' said Samuels. 'You're looking for some people, I understand.'

'Yes,' replied Munro.

They started walking to the front of the airport.

'They got here this morning. They're now at Rawlin's Plantation Inn,' Samuels said. 'Rawlin's is a small, expensive hotel out in the country. It's only got twelve rooms. These people took all the rooms and they're the only people there.'

'OK,' said Munro.

They walked out onto the street. There was a small jeep in front of them.

'I got you a car,' said Samuels. 'Here are the keys and a map.'

'Thanks,' said Munro.

'I wrote my phone number on the map,' said Samuels. 'You can call me. Any time.'

'Thanks,' said Munro again.

* * *

It took Munro forty-five minutes to get to Rawlin's. The road took him up the east of the island. There were fields of sugar on his left, palm trees and the sea on his right.

He found the road up to the hotel and stopped. There was a sign across the road: 'RAWLIN'S PLANTATION INN – OPEN AGAIN FRIDAY'. Today was Wednesday.

Munro looked at the map. It was a kilometre and a half to the hotel.

'Twelve rooms in the hotel, but only four people there,' he thought. 'And the sign says the hotel isn't open. Interesting! They don't want anyone to know they're here – just the hotel workers.'

It was seven o'clock and starting to get dark. Munro got out of the jeep and opened his bag. Quickly he changed his clothes. He put on a black shirt and black jeans. He didn't want anyone to see him. He left the jeep and walked up the road to Rawlin's. Munro loved Caribbean evenings – just nicely warm, after a hot day.

About fifteen metres from the front door of the hotel he stopped behind a tree. The three terrorists and the boy were inside the hotel, in the dining room. There were some tables and chairs outside the front of the hotel. Munro waited behind the tree and watched.

After fifteen minutes the four of them finished dinner and came outside. There was something in Beck's jacket pocket.

'A gun,' thought Munro. He looked at Tajik. There was one in his pocket too.

Salgado sat with the boy. The boy's eyes started to close. Then he opened them again.

'When am I going home?' he asked. 'I want to see my Dad.'

'Tomorrow, maybe.' Salgado smiled at him. 'Your father's going to help us with something first. Then I'm going to take you home.'

'But why am I here?' asked the boy. 'Why am I with you? I don't understand.'

Salgado put a hand on the boy's arm.

'Ask your Dad tomorrow,' she said. 'Everything's going to be OK.'

Salgado got up and went into the hotel. Two minutes later she came out with a yellow drink in her hand. She gave it to the boy.

'Here,' she said. 'Drink this. Banana milk. It's nice.'

The boy drank it.

'Drugs,' thought Munro. 'The boy doesn't know these people, but he's not afraid. It must be because of drugs. That's why he moves slowly and looks half asleep.'

'Why don't you listen to some music?' said Salgado.

'OK.' The boy smiled at Salgado. Then he took out an MP3 player and started listening to it.

Five minutes later a waiter came out with some coffee.

Tajik tried his coffee and stood up angrily.

'This isn't coffee!' he shouted at the waiter. 'It's water. Bring me some coffee!'

'I'm sorry, but …' the waiter began.

Tajik took the front of the waiter's shirt in his hand.

'Sorry?' he shouted. 'I want coffee! Good coffee! Not this!'

Then Salgado stood up.

'Sam! Shut up!' she shouted at Tajik. 'Don't be stupid. Take your hands off that man. The coffee's OK. Sit down, shut up and drink it!'

The waiter looked at Salgado.

'Go,' she said.

The waiter looked at Beck.

'Yes, go!' said Beck. 'All of you. Go and come back tomorrow morning at breakfast time. We don't need anything more tonight.'

The waiter left quickly.

Beck put a hand on Tajik's arm.

'Sit down, Sam,' he said.

Tajik looked down at Beck. Then he sat. He didn't look at Salgado.

'Tajik's a dangerous man,' thought Munro. 'He gets angry very quickly. And about nothing.'

Salgado sat down and looked angrily at Tajik, but she said nothing.

Munro took out his phone. He took some photos of the boy and sent them to Naylor. He also sent an email: 'Wait for my call.'

Then he waited again. No one must see him leave.

At nine o'clock Salgado put her hand on the boy's arm.

'Come on!' she said. 'Time for bed.'

They stood up and went inside. A light came on in a window to the left of the dining room. After a short time the window went dark.

'The boy's room,' thought Munro.

Salgado didn't come outside again.

At nine-fifteen Beck went in. At nine-thirty Tajik looked at his watch. He took his gun out, stood up and started to walk round the hotel.

Munro left quickly. He ran down the road and found his jeep. He called Naylor.

'Did you get the photos?' asked Munro.

'Yes,' replied Naylor. 'Can you get the boy out of the hotel?'

'I can try,' replied Munro. 'But what about the police? Wesley Samuels? Why don't we ask them for help?'

'No police,' said Naylor. 'These people are very dangerous. They don't want to kill the boy, but … you never know. I don't want the police anywhere near the hotel. Not with that boy still there.'

'OK,' replied Munro.

'The boy's name is Jamie Anderson,' said Naylor. 'He was on Tobago with his father. They have a holiday home there. His father is Patrick Anderson, the number one nuclear scientist in the world.'

'Then the terrorists aren't going to want money for the boy, are they?' said Munro.

'No,' replied Naylor. 'I don't think it's going to be money. Just get the boy out of the hotel. Then call Samuels.'

'OK,' said Munro.

'And get him out tonight,' said Naylor.

'Right,' said Munro.

Chapter 4   *Getting into the hotel*

Munro sat in the jeep and thought. Then he went back up to the hotel.

Tajik was still outside the front of the hotel. A light was on over his head. Munro moved very slowly. He made no noise. Away from the front door it was dark. Munro moved near to Tajik behind some flowers. Tajik's gun was on the table next to him.

Tajik looked at his watch. Then he stood up, took his gun and walked round the hotel. He came back to the front and sat down. Munro looked at his watch. It was ten-thirty.

Just then Beck came out again and sat down.

'Is everything OK for tomorrow?' asked Tajik.

'Yes,' answered Beck. 'Anderson is going to email us.'

'And is he going to help us?' asked Tajik.

'He loves his son,' replied Beck.

'And the police?' asked Tajik.

'The police know nothing,' replied Beck. 'Anderson isn't going to tell them anything. He wants his son to live.'

The men didn't speak for a minute. Then Tajik spoke, a smile on his face: 'The woman – she's just here to help with the boy. And she knows too much. What are we going to do with her after this?'

Beck turned fast in his chair. He was angry.

'She's mine,' he said slowly. 'You're not going to do anything with her. She does this job for me. Then she's mine. No girl leaves me and lives.'

Beck stood up and looked down at Tajik.

'I'm going to bed,' he said. 'Don't go to sleep. Maria's coming out at two o'clock. You can sleep then.'

He turned and went back into the hotel. Tajik took his gun off the table and looked at Beck's back. Slowly he put the gun down on the table. Then he turned and smiled – but there was an angry look in his eyes.

'Naylor's right,' thought Munro. 'Tajik is an animal, a very dangerous animal.'

Munro sat behind the flowers and waited and thought.

He wanted to get the boy out of the hotel quickly, without any noise, without any guns or shouting or killing.

He thought about Maria Salgado.

'Yes, she slept with me in Tobago,' he thought. 'But she's not going to help me. She's still a terrorist. She's still dangerous. She doesn't know what Beck thinks about her. But I can't talk to her about it. There's no time.'

Tajik stood up and walked round the hotel again. Munro looked at his watch. 11:00:00. Tajik came back to the front of the hotel. Munro looked at his watch again. It was 11:01:30.

'Ninety seconds,' Munro thought.

By day there were three terrorists and only one of him. But now, at night, two of them were asleep. It wasn't three to one, but one to one.

It took Tajik ninety seconds to walk round the hotel. Munro had ninety seconds to get in, get the boy and get out.

'Can I do it?' thought Munro. 'Yes, I can.'

After half an hour Tajik stood up.

'Now!' thought Munro. 'Ninety seconds.'

Tajik took his gun and started to walk round the hotel. Munro came out from behind the flowers.

Chapter 5   *Too little time*

Munro ran to the front door. He made no noise. He opened the door and went into the hotel.

There were two doors to his left. The second was the boy's room. Munro went inside and quickly closed the door.

Eighty seconds.

It was dark in the room, but Munro could see a little – a bed, a chair, a small table. The boy was in bed, eyes closed.

Munro put a hand on the boy's shoulder.

'Jamie,' he said. 'Come on, Jamie! It's time to get up.'

Nothing.

Seventy seconds.

Munro tried again.

'Come on, Jamie,' he said. 'We need to go. Come on!'

Jamie's eyes moved a little.

'It's the drugs,' thought Munro. 'This isn't going to be easy.'

'Come on, Jamie,' he said.

Sixty seconds.

Jamie's eyes opened. He saw Munro. He started to speak, but Munro put his hand over the boy's mouth.

'Don't talk,' he said. 'I'm taking you home. OK? Do you understand?'

Munro took his hand away.

'Yes,' said Jamie.

'Good,' said Munro. 'Then get out of bed and put some shoes on. Quickly.'

Jamie got out of bed and slowly started to put on his shoes.

Fifty seconds.

'Come on, Jamie!' thought Munro, but he said nothing. Just then he heard a sound. Munro looked at Jamie. He opened his mouth to say something, but the door to Jamie's room started to open. Munro moved quickly behind the door. The light came on.

It was Tajik with his gun in his hand.

Munro moved fast. His left arm went round Tajik's neck. He put one finger of his right hand against Tajik's back. Munro didn't have a gun – but Tajik didn't know that.

'There's a gun in your back,' said Munro. 'Don't speak. Put your gun on the bed.'

Tajik put his gun on the bed. Munro took it. Somewhere in the hotel a door opened and closed. Munro put the gun to Tajik's head. But then Beck was there at the door, with a gun in his hand.

'You can't shoot him and me,' said Beck. 'Put that gun on the bed.'

'What can I do?' thought Munro. 'Nothing.'

He heard Tajik laugh a little.

'Put it down now!' said Beck angrily.

Munro put the gun on the bed and took his arm away from Tajik's neck. He moved back. Tajik turned round and saw Munro for the first time.

'Ah!' he said. 'The man from Tobago. Maria enjoyed playing with you. She didn't tell us, of course, but we knew.' He laughed. 'Now I'm going to enjoy playing with you too.' He took his gun from the bed.

Chapter 6 *Salgado's move*

'Wait,' said Beck to Tajik. He looked at Munro.

'How did you find us?' he asked.

Munro thought quickly. He didn't want to say anything about Naylor or the police.

'The airport in Tobago,' he answered. 'I asked about your plane. They told me you wanted to go to St Kitts. It was easy to find you here – two men, a woman and a boy. It's a small island.'

'And who asked you to find us?' asked Beck. 'The boy's father?'

'Is it important?' asked Munro.

'Maybe it is,' said Beck. 'And then maybe it isn't.'

He laughed.

'You know who the boy's father is?' said Beck.

'Yes,' said Munro.

'Patrick Anderson,' said Beck.

Munro said nothing. He was happy for Beck to talk. It gave him time.

'Professor Patrick Anderson,' said Beck. 'The number one nuclear scientist in the world.'

'Then you're not going to want money from him, are you?' said Munro. 'You're going to want a nuclear …'

'Yes,' said Beck. 'That's just what we want. We're going to be the world's first nuclear terrorists. Things are never going to be the same again – not for the rich, not for the USA, not for Europe, not for the West. We're going to make a new world. Our world. We're going to be famous.'

Beck smiled. His eyes danced.

Tajik laughed.

'What can I do here?' thought Munro. 'I need to get out of here – but how?'

He looked round the room. Beck and Tajik were in front of the door. They had guns. Jamie still looked half asleep.

'You're not working for the boy's father,' said Beck. 'Well, who are you working for? Who knows about us?'

Munro said nothing.

Beck smiled.

'You're English, no?' he said, his eyes cold. 'Then I think you must work for Mr Naylor.'

Again Munro said nothing.

'Yes, I know about Mr Naylor,' said Beck. 'But he can do nothing for you now. You're going to die. The boy is going to die. That woman is going to die. And then we're going to change the world.'

And then he laughed. And Tajik laughed with him.

'Do it,' Beck said to Tajik.

Munro watched the gun in Tajik's hand come up. There was a noise. The noise of a gun, but not Tajik's. Half of Tajik's head turned red. The noise came from behind the two terrorists. Beck started to turn. But it was too late. There was a second noise. Beck's head went back.

Munro didn't move.

Maria Salgado stood in front of him. There was a gun in her hand.

'You heard them,' she said.

'Yes,' said Munro.

'First you, then the boy, then me,' she said.

'Yes,' said Munro.

'Tajik was an animal, but Beck and I … we were friends at one time,' she said. 'Friends for five years. Then I went back to South America.'

'I know,' said Munro.

'Then he asked me to work with him again, but I never thought …' She didn't finish. She just looked down at Beck.

'No,' said Munro.

Salgado looked at Munro again.

'Take the boy. He's yours,' she said. 'Don't try and find me.'

Then she turned and left.

Munro took out his phone.

He called Samuels first, then Naylor.

'I've got the boy,' said Munro.

'Good,' said Naylor. 'Professor Anderson gets to St Kitts at eight o'clock this morning. Samuels can take the boy and give him back to his father. What about the terrorists?'

'Beck and Tajik are dead,' answered Munro.

'Good,' replied Naylor. 'And Salgado?'

'She's not here,' replied Munro. 'I don't know where she is.'

Munro put his phone back in his pocket. He saw the blue lights of two police cars on the road up to the hotel.

'Come on, Jamie,' he said. 'Get that shoe on. It's time to go.'